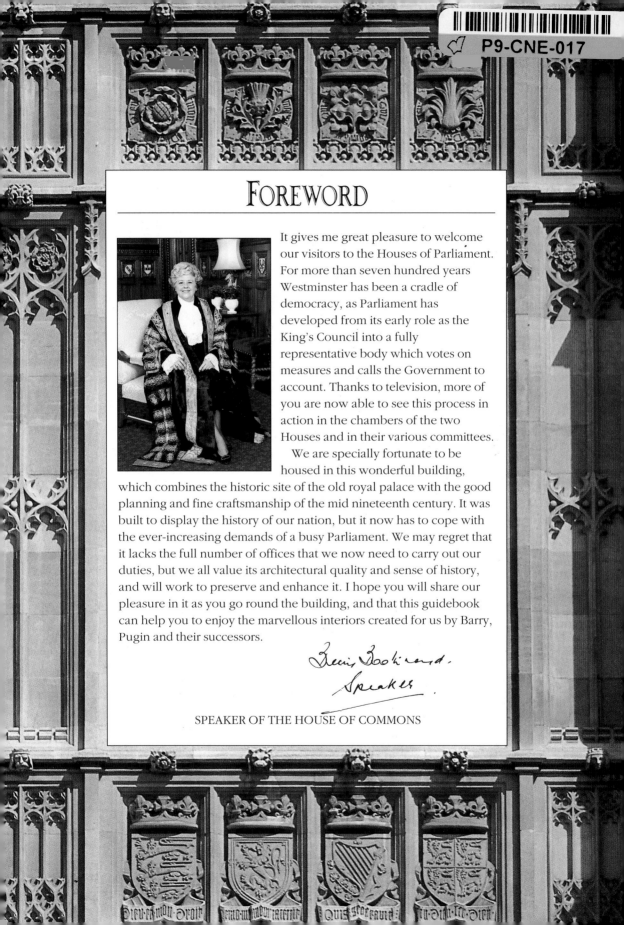

FOREWORD

It gives me great pleasure to welcome our visitors to the Houses of Parliament. For more than seven hundred years Westminster has been a cradle of democracy, as Parliament has developed from its early role as the King's Council into a fully representative body which votes on measures and calls the Government to account. Thanks to television, more of you are now able to see this process in action in the chambers of the two Houses and in their various committees. We are specially fortunate to be housed in this wonderful building, which combines the historic site of the old royal palace with the good planning and fine craftsmanship of the mid nineteenth century. It was built to display the history of our nation, but it now has to cope with the ever-increasing demands of a busy Parliament. We may regret that it lacks the full number of offices that we now need to carry out our duties, but we all value its architectural quality and sense of history, and will work to preserve and enhance it. I hope you will share our pleasure in it as you go round the building, and that this guidebook can help you to enjoy the marvellous interiors created for us by Barry, Pugin and their successors.

Betty Boothroyd.
Speaker.

SPEAKER OF THE HOUSE OF COMMONS

The Old Palace

The New Palace of Westminster – the correct name of the Houses of Parliament – stands on a historic riverside site which links it with the origins of Parliament and the ancient palace of the Norman kings.

This originally marshy spot was first used by Canute for a royal palace, but it was Edward the Confessor who established the medieval building now known as the Old Palace, to be close to the Abbey of St Peter at Westminster which he refounded. The Old Palace was both a royal residence and a meeting place of parliaments; it was the principal residence of the kings of England until 1532, when Henry VIII moved to Whitehall Palace and St James's Palace. No longer a royal residence, the Palace of Westminster nevertheless remains a royal palace to this day.

The Old Palace was built as a residence for the King and his court, and as a setting for state ceremonial. Over the centuries it was rebuilt and extended, but its most important structure remained Westminster Hall, which still stands today. This was the meeting place of the King's Council, a body later enlarged to include knights of the shires and burgesses from the towns during the struggle for power between

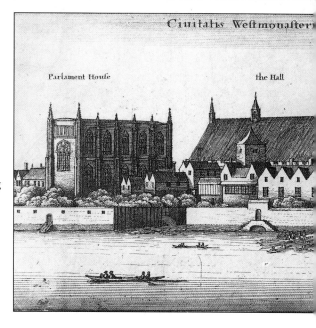

Henry III and Simon de Montfort. The Great Parliament of 1265, which met in this hall, has been seen as the origin of the modern Parliament.

The separation of the Commons (the knights and burgesses) from the Lords (the nobles and prelates) seems to have begun about 1332. The Commons met in parts of the palace or in the chapter house or refectory of the abbey until in 1547 the private chapel of the palace – St Stephen's Chapel, on the site of the present

LEFT **Sir Christopher Wren made changes to St Stephen's Chapel in 1707, inserting three round-headed windows, adding panelling and galleries and lowering the roof. Subsequent architects tried to maximise the space in the long narrow chamber, but the seating arrangements remained rather crowded, with parallel rows of benches facing each other. This probably influenced the present seating plan of the Commons.**

LEFT **Wenceslaus Hollar's view of the Old Palace from the river in 1647 shows St Stephen's Chapel – described as the 'Parlament House' – prominent among a muddle of lesser buildings. Seen here in front of Westminster Abbey is the clock tower built in New Palace Yard in 1365 close to where 'Big Ben' now stands.**

RIGHT **The haphazard nature of the old palace compared with the symmetry of the new is shown on this plan.**

☐ Old Palace
── New Palace
──► N

St Stephen's Hall – was secularised and given to the Commons as their first permanent meeting place. The Commons adapted it to their needs, installing the Speaker's chair in front of the altar and using the chapel stalls for seats.

Until 1801 the Lords met in the Parliament Chamber, at the southern end of the Old Palace. It was beneath this chamber that Guy Fawkes and his fellow conspirators placed barrels of gunpowder in 1605, an act of treason which led to their execution in Old Palace Yard.

After the Union with Ireland in 1801 the Lords, seeking more space, moved into the Court of Requests, to the south of Westminster Hall where the statue of Richard I now stands. The Lords remained there, and the Commons in St Stephen's Chapel, until the night of 16 October 1834 when the Old Palace went up in flames. The overheating of a House of Lords furnace filled with Exchequer tally sticks used for keeping accounts led to a massive blaze which destroyed almost all of the rambling medieval building.

RIGHT **The 1834 fire destroyed nearly all of the Old Palace. This view shows St Stephen's Chapel – the meeting place of the Commons – in the centre of the river front. To the left are the buildings used by the Lords, and to the right the Speaker's House with the mass of Westminster Hall rising behind it.**

THE NEW PALACE

A new Palace of Westminster, much more magnificent and carefully planned for its purpose, was to rise on the site of the old building, whose unsuitability as the seat of Parliament had long been recognised.

The fire provided an opportunity to create a new building which could be a symbol of the spirit of parliamentary reform (the 1832 Reform Act had just been passed), a monument to the history of the nation and a building providing the comforts available in the mid nineteenth century. A competition was held, specifying a design in either the gothic or Elizabethan style. Out of ninety-seven entries the winner was Charles Barry, who chose the Perpendicular gothic style to harmonise with Westminster Abbey's Henry VII Chapel opposite. He created a functional secular palace combining practical arrangements with an extraordinary complexity of ornament, aiming to achieve 'a sculptured memorial of our national history'.

ABOVE **Barry designed the buildings of the New Palace around a series of courtyards, above which rise the central tower and the clock tower in this view looking north. The Commons' chamber is in the block between the two towers.**

SIR CHARLES BARRY

Born in Bridge Street, Westminster, the son of a stationer, Sir Charles Barry (1795–1860) was already a leading architect when he won the competition of 1836 to design the New Palace. The heavy demands of the work at Westminster, probably exacerbated by his own perfectionist approach, caused him to complain that he had been obliged to give up more than two-thirds of a lucrative practice. He was knighted in 1852, shortly after the new Lords' and Commons' chambers had come into permanent use. Other important works by him are the Travellers' Club and the Reform Club in London built in the classical style, and Halifax Town Hall in the gothic style. This statue by J.H. Foley, showing Barry studying plans for the New Palace, is on the staircase leading up from the Lower Waiting Hall.

BELOW **The most unified design of the New Palace is the east front, which has an unbroken line of large pinnacles stretching along the river for 872 feet (265 m). Barry raised the central part of this façade to provide more interest. Below the east front is the paved terrace beside the river which is popular with MPs during the summer.**

LEFT **This equestrian statue of Richard I by Baron Marochetti was erected in Old Palace Yard in 1860.**

RIGHT **The highly decorated exterior includes lettering, heraldic panels and over 300 statues of kings, queens and saints installed within a picturesque but regular gothic framework.**

His design had a pioneering emphasis on the use of space, locating the two chambers and all the main rooms on the principal floor. Its circulation areas and public rooms work as successfully today as when they were designed, particularly as a result of the symmetrical layout planned around the Central Lobby and along the river front. At either end Barry placed imposing towers which he set back from the river. In the south the Victoria Tower rises above Millbank, and to the north the Clock Tower with its famous hour bell Big Ben dominates New Palace Yard. Westminster Hall, which survived the fire, was incorporated into the scheme.

The interiors of the New Palace were developed in collaboration with A.W.N. Pugin, whose inventive genius for adapting gothic forms created the elaborate furniture, carvings and fittings. The partnership of these two men produced the first great Gothic Revival public building. Barry created the overall design of the palace and dealt with its planning and construction – a great technical feat in itself. Pugin supplied a flood of drawings for every part of the building, which Barry did not hesitate to

ABOVE **The Victoria Tower rises 323 feet (98 m) to the base of the flagstaff, from which the Union Jack is flown on days when Parliament is sitting and on some special occasions. The flag can be as large as 36 feet (11 m) by 18 feet (5.5 m) – one of three sizes are flown according to the strength of the wind – and is replaced by the Royal Standard when the Queen comes to open Parliament at the beginning of each session. The tower contains the records of Parliament, including the master copies of Acts of Parliament since 1497.**

ABOVE **Each of the Clock Tower's four vast clock faces (the inside of one is shown here) is 23 feet (7 m) in diameter and the figures are 2 feet (0.6 m) long.**

BELOW **Big Ben, the clock's hour bell, was probably named after a champion boxer of the period rather than the First Commissioner of Works, Sir Benjamin Hall.**

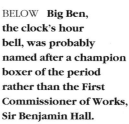

ABOVE **The Clock Tower is famous for its mighty clock, which began its service in 1859 and overcame some early problems to become a reliable timekeeper and a much-loved landmark. A light shines from the top of the tower when either House is sitting at night.**

A.W.N. PUGIN

The son of a French emigré architect and artist, Augustus Welby Northmore Pugin (1812–52) began designing furniture and silver at the age of fifteen, but was still virtually unknown when he helped Barry with the drawings for the competition design. By 1844, when he returned to assist at Westminster, he was a well-known architect and theorist of the gothic style. Converted to Roman Catholicism in 1835, he worked hard at designing churches and houses in addition to his labours on the New Palace. This overwork probably contributed to his apparent mental illness and premature death. The portrait by J.R. Herbert, in a frame designed by Pugin himself, hangs in the Pugin Room, restored and renamed in his honour in 1978, where MPs entertain their guests.

alter with an eye to the scale and overall effect. After Pugin's death in 1852 his designs continued to be used. Barry died in 1860 and work on the palace was continued by his son Edward Middleton Barry.

The building covers an area of eight acres (3.2 hectares), and was not finished until the 1870s at a total cost of over two million pounds. It has undergone changes ever since. Offices needed to be created out of the spacious residences originally included for the senior officers of Parliament. In the process many fittings and decorations were removed or obscured, particularly during the 1920s and 1930s when Pugin's style went out of fashion. Luckily, painted ceilings were often only covered over, and records of the original wallpapers and other designs can be traced. A steady programme of work in the last twenty years has recreated the richly decorated interiors which comprise many of the 1,100 rooms in daily working use throughout the palace.

ABOVE **Old Palace Yard is overlooked by the west front of the palace and Barry's great south window of Westminster Hall.**

SOME STATISTICS

Length of river front	*872 ft (265 m)*
Area of site	*8 acres (3.2 hectares) (approx)*
Staircases	*100*
Length of passageways	*3 miles (4.8 km) (approx)*
Rooms	*1,100*
Commons' chamber (floor)	*68 ft x 46 ft (20.7 m x 14 m)*
Lords' chamber	*80 ft x 45 ft (24.4 m x 13.7 m)*
St Stephen's Hall	*95 ft x 30 ft (29 m x 9.1 m)*
Westminster Hall	*240 ft x 68 ft (73 m x 20.7 m)*
Height of Clock Tower	*316 ft (96 m)*
Height of Victoria Tower	*323 ft (98 m)*

The great clock

Hands: minute (copper)	*14 ft (4.3 m)*
hour (gunmetal)	*9 ft (2.7 m)*
Glass panes in each face	*312*
Pendulum	*14 ft 5 in (4.4 m)*
Weight of Big Ben	*13 tons 10cwt 99lb (13.75 tonnes)*

THE ROYAL PROCESSIONAL ROUTE

Inside the palace the level of decoration varies depending on the ceremonial importance of each area. Thus the grandest interiors were created in the Lords' chamber and the suite of rooms which form the royal processional route for the State Opening. For this purpose the architect preferred halls to staircases.

The pageantry of the State Opening begins as the royal carriage comes through the arch at the base of the Victoria Tower. Here the Queen enters the palace and climbs the **Royal Staircase** with its unbroken ascent of wide low treads. The procession then reaches the landing called the **Norman Porch**, so named because there had been plans to instal statues of Norman sovereigns here. It is dominated by an atmospheric portrait of Queen Victoria.

The **Queen's Robing Room**, the next room in the Queen's progress, is in the centre of the south front of the palace. This elaborately decorated room contains a series of frescos based on the story of King Arthur. The artist, William Dyce, worked on them between 1848 and 1864, painting only in the summer because of problems of getting the wet plaster to dry. The Arthurian legend is also used for the carved bas-reliefs which are set into the linenfold panelling. At the end of the room is a Chair of State designed by E.M. Barry, who also designed the ornate fireplace. The Robing Room was used as the House of Lords between 1941 and 1951, when the Commons moved into the Lords' chamber after their own chamber had been destroyed in wartime bombing. Since then it has been used for its original purpose, as the apartment where the sovereign puts on the Imperial State Crown and parliamentary robes.

When the Queen is ready the double doors are opened and her procession moves into the **Royal Gallery**. This vast room, some 100 feet (30 m) long, is lined with two historical scenes, of the death of Nelson at Trafalgar and the meeting of Wellington and Blucher at Waterloo. Plans for other frescos were abandoned, and portraits of kings and queens since George I

ABOVE   **At the State Opening the Queen processes through the Royal Gallery wearing the Imperial State Crown, escorted by the great officers of state.**

BELOW   **Portrait busts of peers who were prime ministers now occupy the pedestals in the Norman Porch which were intended for statues of Norman sovereigns.**

LEFT The Chair of State in the Robing Room does not follow any of Pugin's surviving designs, and was probably designed by E.M. Barry in the 1860s.

ABOVE At the end of the Robing Room the Chair of State stands in front of a fine needlework panel embroidered with the royal arms by the Royal School of Needlework in 1856. The portraits of Queen Victoria and Prince Albert are by Winterhalter and the large fresco by William Dyce depicts Sir Gawain swearing to be merciful.

RIGHT The fireplace by E.M. Barry installed in the Robing Room in 1864–6 demonstrates the greater richness of style that he favoured. The gilded statues of St George and St Michael were added in 1870.

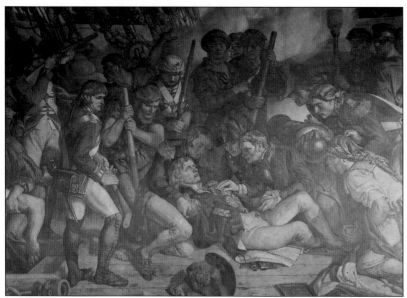

LEFT **In the Royal Gallery the two huge pictures of military victories, of which a detail of the painting representing the death of Nelson at Trafalgar is shown here, were painted between 1858 and 1865 by Daniel Maclise, who was paid £3,500 for each work. They each measure 45 ft by 12 ft (13.7 m by 3.7 m) and successfully combine meticulous detail with an epic scale.**

BELOW **Originally the Royal Gallery was to have had a lower ceiling but in the final stages of his design the architect decided to raise the roof to make the room more impressive. Apart from the State Opening and occasional parliamentary ceremonies, the gallery is not greatly used. On display in it are the death warrant of Charles I and other parliamentary records.**

ABOVE **Dominating the Prince's Chamber is the statue of the young Queen Victoria, by John Gibson. Controversy has always surrounded the scale of the work, and the flanking statues of Justice and Mercy were banished to storage in Woolwich from 1955 until 1976 when a change in public taste caused them to be reinstated.**

RIGHT **The Tudor portraits in the Prince's Chamber were painted in oil on panels in 1854–60 by students from the Royal School of Art, but were based on the best contemporary sources. This one of Henry VIII used a half-length portrait by Holbein as its main authority.**

now cover the walls. Other decorations include four pairs of gilded royal statues, and large Tudor roses in the ceiling panels and on the archways; these are a favourite emblem throughout the palace. The room is occasionally used for parliamentary ceremonies, including the reception of visiting statesmen from abroad.

From the Royal Gallery the Queen's procession passes into the **Prince's Chamber**. The decoration of this room is based on a Tudor theme, and includes full-length portraits of Henry VIII and his six wives and other leading figures of the period. The room also contains a large neo-classical statue of Queen Victoria, two fine octagonal tables and a set of lion-headed chairs designed by Pugin in his grandest manner.

THE HOUSE OF LORDS

The decorative scheme in the palace reaches its climax in the chamber of the House of Lords. Here the whole Parliament – Sovereign, Lords and Commons – assembles for the State Opening.

A richly carved and gilded canopy in three compartments emphasises the importance of the Queen's throne, and the rest of the chamber is decorated with equal richness. It contains sumptuous examples of nineteenth-century craftsmanship in wood and metal, including the great standing brass candelabra on either side of the throne. High on the walls are eighteen large bronze statues of barons and prelates who witnessed the signing of Magna Carta, and in the arched recesses large frescos extol the virtues of justice, religion and chivalry. The elaborate panelled ceiling was restored in 1980–84 after a small part of it fell into the chamber during a late night sitting. Investigation revealed that much of the wood was fixed only with glue, which had dried out over the years.

ABOVE **The throne in the House of Lords was based by Pugin on the medieval Coronation Chair in Westminster Abbey. A second throne, a slightly smaller copy made for Queen Alexandra in 1901, is installed when needed for the Duke of Edinburgh.**

THE STATE OPENING OF PARLIAMENT

After the Queen's ceremonial procession into the House of Lords, the Gentleman Usher of the Black Rod is sent to the House of Commons. Their door is first slammed in his face, to symbolise the Commons' claim to exclude the Sovereign from their deliberations. Black Rod knocks three times on the door and is finally admitted to deliver his message commanding the attendance of 'this honourable House' in the House of Lords.

The Speaker then leads MPs in procession across the Central Lobby to the Bar of the Lords' chamber from where they hear the Queen read the 'Gracious Speech'. This is handed to Her Majesty by the Lord Chancellor, and announces the Government's programme for the forthcoming session.

RIGHT **A State Opening by James I in 1605 was the intended target of the Gunpowder Plot. The cellars of the House of Lords have ever since been checked by the Yeomen of the Guard on the eve of each State Opening.**

ABOVE **Presiding over the Lords in session is the Lord Chancellor. He sits on the woolsack, which is stuffed with wool, and is thought to have been first placed in the Lords during the reign of Edward III. It symbolised the importance of wool to the wealth of the nation. Apart from the Lord Chancellor and the bishops, peers do not wear special costume except at the State Opening or when taking part in the introduction of newly created peers.**

It is in this magnificent setting that the peers conduct their business. Like the House of Commons, the House of Lords holds general debates, puts questions to ministers (of whom about twenty are members of the House) and considers legislation. Its procedure and practices differ in detail from those of the Commons, and its powers over legislation are qualified: the Lords may not amend 'money bills', and they can only delay other bills passed by the Commons for an effective period of thirteen months.

The House of Lords also has a judicial function as the final Court of Appeal for England, Wales and Northern Ireland, and, in civil matters only, for Scotland. Such business is conducted by the Lords of Appeal, who include senior judges specially appointed to the Lords.

The House is presided over by the Lord Chancellor, who sits on the woolsack in front of the throne. The other peers sit on the red padded benches, with the Government party sitting on the throne's right hand. In former times

BELOW **Carvings such as this lion and unicorn in the Lords' chamber show the capabilities of craftsmen of the 1840s. Barry and Pugin used a large team of carpenters, and relied on close colleagues such as Hardman for metal-work, Crace for painting and Minton for tiles.**

RIGHT **The Lords first occupied their magnificent chamber in 1847, when *The Builder* magazine enthused that 'the whole glitters with colours and gilding – carvings in stone, stained glass, encaustic tiles, and fine work in metal'.**

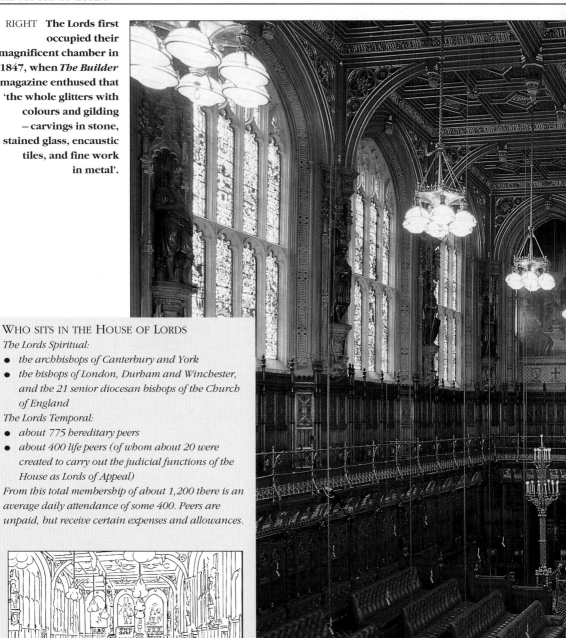

WHO SITS IN THE HOUSE OF LORDS

The Lords Spiritual:

- *the archbishops of Canterbury and York*
- *the bishops of London, Durham and Winchester, and the 21 senior diocesan bishops of the Church of England*

The Lords Temporal:

- *about 775 hereditary peers*
- *about 400 life peers (of whom about 20 were created to carry out the judicial functions of the House as Lords of Appeal)*

From this total membership of about 1,200 there is an average daily attendance of some 400. Peers are unpaid, but receive certain expenses and allowances.

1 Throne. 2 Woolsack. 3 Bishops. 4 Liberal Democrats. 5 Government. 6 Opposition. 7 Clerks.

this side belonged to the Lords Spiritual, and still contains a special bench to accommodate the bishops (easily identified by its armrests, not provided on the other benches). The cross-benches are at the north end of the chamber, in front of the Bar of the House where the Speaker and MPs stand at the State Opening, and from where barristers make their speeches when the chamber is used for judicial sittings. Behind it lies the archway leading to the Peers Lobby.

The area of the palace occupied by the House of Lords includes committee rooms, libraries, dining rooms and offices. Many of these rooms have been altered little since their completion, and are furnished with over 1,100 pieces of original furniture.

LEFT **The fine pair of studded brass gates in the Peers Lobby, which lead into the Lords' chamber, have been much admired ever since the building was completed. Brass panels of tracery combine with emblems of state and monarchy in a triumph of heraldic display, which Pugin checked by constructing a full-scale model in wax and wood. The gates were made to his designs by the Birmingham firm of John Hardman which he persuaded to move from button making to metal working in the medieval style.**

LEFT **Pugin and Hardman worked together on the central feature of the Peers Lobby floor, which includes a Tudor rose of Derbyshire marbles. Pugin insisted on deep cutting of the decorated brass plates which has ensured that the pattern remains clear.**

ABOVE **One of Pugin's heraldic tiles made by Minton for the floor of the Peers Lobby.**

ABOVE **This is one of the four rooms on the river front which accommodate the House of Lords Library. Its rich interiors include various pieces of furniture designed by Pugin, of which some 325 distinct types have been identified in the rooms of the palace occupied by the Lords.**

RIGHT **This large committee room off the Peers Lobby is called the Moses Room after the fresco of Moses bringing down the Tablets of the Law from Mount Sinai, by J.R. Herbert, completed in 1864.**

THE CENTRAL LOBBY

The hub of the building is the Central Lobby, a busy meeting place where people come to 'lobby' their MPs. It is sited along the central axis between the Commons' and Lords' chambers, and on the Commons' side is a desk manned by police and attendants from where constituents can send in a 'green card' to contact their representatives.

Archways lead off to the two chambers and to their galleries, as well as to the Lower Waiting Hall where a marble bust of Oliver Cromwell is prominently on display. Beyond the hall, along the river front, are the libraries and dining rooms

ABOVE **The mosaic picture of St David was the second such picture to be installed in the Central Lobby. Like the picture of St George, its design was by Sir George Poynter and its execution by the Venice firm of Salviati.**

LEFT **Designs in the fine mosaic ceiling of the Central Lobby include the English Tudor rose, the Scottish thistle, the Irish shamrock, the Welsh harp, the French fleur-de-lis and the portcullis, now familiar in its crowned form as the emblem of Parliament. The portcullis was a royal symbol of the Tudors, adopted by Charles Barry as his identifying mark for the palace competition and used extensively in the decoration of the building.**

available to MPs and to the right an elegant gothic staircase leads to the committee rooms. Before the start of each day's sitting of the Commons the Speaker processes through this hall and the Central Lobby to the cry of 'Hats off, strangers!' from the police.

The vast octagon of the Central Lobby has a vaulted stone roof which was decorated with mosaics in 1868–9 by E.M. Barry. Over the four archways are panels depicting the patron saints, a series which was begun in 1870 with St George for England, continued in 1898 with St David for Wales, and after a long pause benefactions enabled the panels of St Andrew for Scotland and St Patrick for Ireland to be installed in 1922–4. The mosaic decoration was intended to make the Central Lobby less gloomy, and E.M. Barry claimed that his additions had achieved a 'general cheerfulness and lightness' which is undoubtedly increased by the great chandelier dating from 1854 made to Pugin's design. Pugin also designed the encaustic tiles in the floor which were made by Minton, and which include a Latin text from Psalm 127 which reads 'Except the Lord build the house, they labour in vain that build it'.

ABOVE **William Gladstone, the 'grand old man' of Victorian politics, is portrayed by one of four large marble statues of nineteenth-century statesmen in the Central Lobby. The statue was sculpted by F.W. Pomeroy.**

LEFT **The Central Lobby's decoration was left unfinished until 1868–9, when E.M. Barry supervised the present scheme.**

Many historical scenes cover the corridor walls in this part of the palace. A scheme to decorate the walls throughout the building with narrative painting was first drawn up by a Fine Art Commission established in 1841 with Prince Albert as its chairman. Not all of its decisions were implemented, and many pictures have disintegrated or faded because artists were encouraged to use fresco (powdered pigments applied directly to wet plaster) rather than oil. However, a scheme of subjects was agreed for the different parts of the palace, and this has been complemented by subsequent additions.

BELOW **Scenes of the Tudor period were installed in 1910 in the East Corridor which leads to the Lower Waiting Hall. This colourful fresco by H.A. Payne illustrates a scene from Shakespeare's *Henry VI Part I* showing the origin of the badges of Lancaster and York: Richard Plantagenet plucking a white rose for the Yorkists and the Earl of Somerset a red rose for Lancaster, in the Temple Gardens. Payne was chosen by the donor of the painting, Earl Beauchamp, who had used the artist to decorate the famous Arts and Crafts chapel at his country house, Madresfield Court.**

LEFT **C.W. Cope was commissioned to paint a series of murals in the Peers Corridor between 1856 and 1866 on the struggle between Parliament and Crown in the Stuart period. The artist chose to include the embarkation of the Pilgrim Fathers for New England in 1620.**

LEFT **Latimer preaches before Edward VI at St Paul's Cross, a fresco by Ernest Brand in the series of scenes of the Tudor period in the East Corridor. Its style reflects the conception of the series as historical illustrations, rather than history painting in the grand manner. All the paintings in this series were donated by Liberal peers.**

RIGHT **The scenes of the Stuart period include the confrontation in 1642 when Speaker Lenthall asserted the privileges of the House of Commons when Charles I came to arrest five members for treason: 'May it please Your Majesty, I have neither eyes to see, nor tongue to speak in this place, but as the House is pleased to direct me . . .' This was the last time a reigning monarch entered the House.**

THE HOUSE OF COMMONS

It is in the House of Commons that political argument and power is centred. A General Election determines the choice of political party to form a government, and its existence depends on maintaining the support of a majority in the Commons. The Government's policies are explained or criticised in debates and at question time, bills (draft laws) are considered, levels of taxation decided and expenditure voted for the running of the country. Most Government ministers (usually all but two of the Cabinet of about twenty, and sixty out of the eighty other ministers) are drawn from this House.

The Commons' chamber was rebuilt in 1945–50 after it and its lobbies were seriously damaged in an air raid on 10 May 1941. In the Commons, or Members, Lobby the archway into

ABOVE **The Speaker is elected by MPs to preside over the Commons, and ceases to belong to a political party after election. The term 'Speaker' derives from the earlier role of spokesman for the Commons in its exchanges with the king. Here the Speaker, wearing her ceremonial robe and accompanied by Black Rod, leads MPs through the Members Lobby to the Lords to hear the Queen's Speech at the State Opening of Parliament.**

REPORTING AND BROADCASTING OF PARLIAMENT

Until the late eighteenth century the House of Commons firmly discouraged the reporting of its proceedings, but the practice came to be accepted and in 1803 press reporters were given a reserved part of the gallery. Reports of debates appeared in William Cobbett's Parliamentary Debates *which were taken over by Thomas Hansard in 1812, so starting the use of the name* Hansard, *an operation run by the House itself since 1909. The verbatim report of proceedings up to about 11 pm is available the next morning. A separate series prepared by staff of the House of Lords covers debates in that House.*

Permanent sound broadcasting of Parliament began in 1978, and television broadcasting in 1986 in the Lords and in 1990 in the Commons. Use is made of remote-control cameras operated from a control room, and coverage includes the work of parliamentary committees.

Charles Dickens worked as a reporter in the gallery for a time in 1832, and described the experience in *Sketches by Boz*.

WHO SITS WHERE IN THE COMMONS

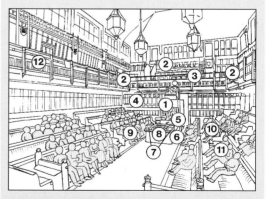

1 The Speaker. 2 Press galleries. 3 Hansard reporters.
4 Government officials' box. 5 Clerks of the House.
6 Table of the House. 7 Despatch boxes. 8 Mace.
9 Government. 10 Opposition. 11 Liberal Democrats.
12 Members' galleries.

RIGHT In the Members Lobby the archway of damaged stonework retained from the old chamber is flanked by statues of wartime prime ministers – Winston Churchill by Oscar Nemon, and David Lloyd George by Uli Nimptsh. A snuff box, traditionally provided for the use of MPs, is kept in the doorkeeper's chair to the right of the arch.

BELOW The post-war rebuilding of the Commons' chamber did not reproduce the original, in use from 1850 to 1941, which had been similar in style to the Lords' chamber but without the paintings or sculpture. Instead, Sir Giles Gilbert Scott chose a simplified gothic style in lighter coloured oak.

RIGHT **The Commons' chamber is here filled with MPs waiting for the arrival of Black Rod to summon them to the Lords at the State Opening of Parliament. The mace can be seen in position on the table. The red stripes in the carpet mark the traditional separation of two swords' lengths between the two sides of the House.**

LEFT **The elaborate silver gilt mace is the symbol of the authority delegated to the Commons by the Sovereign and the emblem of their power and privileges. The present mace has been used by the Commons since the end of the reign of George III. It stays on the table throughout each sitting except when the House goes into committee (for detailed examination of bills), when the Serjeant at Arms places it on supports underneath.**

ABOVE **MPs vote by going into either the 'Aye' lobby or the 'No' lobby, where they give their names to the clerks sitting at the high desks and are counted by tellers as they file out. They have eight minutes to reach the lobbies before the doors are locked. When all MPs have voted, the tellers from both sides report their figures to the Chair.**

DAILY TIMETABLE OF THE HOUSE OF COMMONS

2.30 pm (10 am Wednesdays) The Speaker arrives in the chamber after a procession from the Speaker's House via the Lower Waiting Hall and Central Lobby

The Speaker's Chaplain leads the House in prayers

(10.05 am–2.30 pm Wednesdays: short adjournment debates on subjects chosen by backbenchers)

2.35–3.30 pm Questions to ministers (based on a rota of departments)

(3.15–3.30 pm Tuesdays and Thursdays: questions to the Prime Minister)

3.30 pm Private Notice (emergency) questions to ministers, statements by ministers and points of order to the Speaker

3.30 pm (or later) Main business of the day begins

10 pm (or later) Other items

Last half-hour of sitting Adjournment debate on a subject chosen by a backbencher

The average length of a daily sitting is currently 8 hours 23 minutes. On Fridays the House meets at 9.30 am, does not usually take questions to ministers, and is likely to adjourn at 3 pm or shortly after.

the chamber incorporates stones from the original arch. It is flanked by statues of Churchill and Lloyd George, and the lobby also has statues of other statesmen – Attlee, Joseph Chamberlain, Balfour, Asquith and Disraeli – as well as message boards for MPs, their post office and the window of the vote office which supplies them with parliamentary papers.

Sir Giles Gilbert Scott's designs for the Commons' chamber repeated the gothic style of the old chamber but in a simplified manner. It was decided to use the floor plan of the old chamber but to enlarge the galleries to provide more seating. Even so there are still only seats for some 420 MPs out of a total of 651, and when the chamber is full members have to find standing room or sit in the gangways. The refusal to enlarge the chamber was a deliberate

and successful attempt to retain a degree of intimacy for the many smaller debates when only a handful of MPs are present. Backbench members speak from their places, but spokesmen for the Government or official Opposition can put their notes on the despatch boxes on the table.

The furniture in the new chamber was given by members of the Commonwealth. Galleries above the Speaker's chair are for the press, and those opposite for 'distinguished strangers', peers, diplomats and the public. On either side of the chamber are the division lobbies used for voting. Other rooms nearby include the long suite of comfortable rooms overlooking the river which house the Commons Library and the members' and strangers' dining rooms.

ABOVE **Purpose-built accommodation for the Commons Library was created in the New Palace. This spacious room with its writing tables and deep armchairs retains much of the atmosphere of a nineteenth-century club.**

LEFT **Parliamentary committees meet in the committee rooms on the first and second floors of the palace, overlooking the river. They are small groups of members appointed by each House on the basis of party balance. In the Commons, standing committees consider most bills in detail, and in both Houses select committees inquire into specific matters. Some of the most active are the investigative select committees of the Commons that scrutinise the work and policy of the principal Government departments.**

THE PARLIAMENTARY YEAR

A parliament lasts up to five years, and its term is divided into a number of sessions. These normally last twelve months and start with the State Opening by the Queen in early November. The two Houses sit until Christmas, then again from early January to mid/late July, with recesses of 10–14 days at Easter and over the spring bank holiday. After a longer recess of 10–12 weeks in the summer Parliament resumes for 2–3 weeks in October, and is then 'prorogued', or suspended, until the cycle begins again with a new State Opening. On average it sits for about 160 to 170 days in a normal year.

Parliament comes to an end when it is dissolved by the Queen on the advice of the Prime Minister. A General Election then selects the 651 members of the House of Commons of the new parliament, and members of the House of Lords receive a fresh writ of summons to attend their House.

Westminster Hall and St Stephen's Hall

Westminster Hall, the huge hall of the medieval palace, survived the 1834 fire largely undamaged and was incorporated into the design of the New Palace. The architect also kept the original ground plan of St Stephen's Chapel, which had been the Commons' chamber for nearly 300 years, and on it built a new vaulted hall which has become the main public approach to both Houses of Parliament.

The walls of **St Stephen's Hall** are covered with a series of large murals on the theme 'The Building of Britain', installed in 1927. But perhaps of greatest interest are the brass studs set in the floor near the steps to the

ABOVE   **In the 'Building of Britain' series in St Stephen's Hall, Vivian Forbes depicted an incident in 1523 when Sir Thomas More, as Speaker, refused to grant Cardinal Wolsey a subsidy for the King without due debate by the Commons.**

LEFT   **St Stephen's Hall is lined with statues of leading statesmen who were distinguished debaters in the old Commons' chamber. They cover a historic period of nearly three centuries and include Walpole, Chatham, Burke, Fox and Pitt.**

RIGHT   **The quiet emptiness of Westminster Hall today contrasts with its earlier existence as the Great Hall of the king's palace, and the centre of the courts of justice. In retaining the hall Barry opened up its south wall with a high arch to create St Stephen's Porch. Here he repeated the great window from that end of the hall, and built a wide flight of steps which serve as a useful dais for ceremonial events.**

LEFT **Coronation banquets were held in Westminster Hall until the reign of George IV, which was the last occasion when the King's Champion rode his horse into the hall and challenged anyone to dispute his master's right to succeed. This print shows *The Bringing Up of the Second Course* on that occasion, on 19 July 1821.**

FAMOUS EVENTS IN WESTMINSTER HALL

Tried and condemned to death:

1305	*Sir William Wallace*
1535	*Sir Thomas More*
1551	*'Protector' Somerset*
1606	*Guy Fawkes*
1641	*The Earl of Strafford*
1649	*Charles I*

After his capture during the Civil War Charles I was tried in Westminster Hall and beheaded on a scaffold outside the Banqueting House.

1653	*Oliver Cromwell took the oath as Lord Protector*
1788–95	*Warren Hastings impeached and acquitted*

Lying in state:

1898	*William Gladstone*
1910	*Edward VII*
1952	*George VI*
1953	*Queen Mary*
1965	*Sir Winston Churchill*

Central Lobby which mark the position of the Speaker's chair and clerks' table in the old Commons' chamber.

Alterations to **Westminster Hall** were limited to a remodelling of the south end to incorporate the hall into the main public approach to the building. The great south window was reglazed after bomb damage in the Second World War and contains memorials to members of both Houses who were killed in the conflict.

The structure is basically the Great Hall which William Rufus built for his Palace of Westminster in 1097–9. It was remodelled in 1394–9 by Richard II, who embellished it with the great north and south windows and statues of Saxon kings, some of which remain on display. The rebuilding was the work of Henry Yevele, the architect of Westminster Abbey, and Hugh Herland, who was responsible for the massive hammerbeam roof with its carved angels.

Westminster Hall played an important role as the place to obtain justice; by the end of the thirteenth century it contained the courts of Common Pleas, the King's Bench and Chancery.

ABOVE **The Crypt Chapel's alabaster and marble font is set in an ornate octagonal baptistry.**

Courts continued in the hall until 1825, when they moved into a new building along its west wall designed by Sir John Soane. This survived the 1834 fire, and was demolished only in 1882 after the construction of the new Royal Courts of Justice in the Strand.

Brass plates set in the floor record some of the many state trials held in the hall as well as the lying in state of monarchs and their consorts in more recent times. Although other great parliamentary and royal ceremonies take place here periodically, the hall usually stands damp and empty as a gloomy but impressive reminder of the medieval palace.

A door from Westminster Hall leads down to the **Chapel of St Mary Undercroft**, which was begun in 1292 and completed in the early fourteenth century. Its stonework had to be entirely renewed after the 1834 fire, and its restoration was completed in the 1860s under the supervision of E.M. Barry. The Crypt Chapel, as it is called, is now used by members of both Houses and their families for marriages and christenings.

ABOVE **Restoration of the Crypt Chapel produced this glorious High Victorian interior enriched with painted roof panels, stained glass, florid ironwork and, as in so much of the palace, wonderful tile designs on floors and walls.**

BELOW **The restored medieval roof bosses depict the martyrdom of saints. Here St Lawrence is burned to death on a gridiron.**

31

THE SPEAKER'S HOUSE

The Speaker's House has some of the most splendid rooms in the New Palace. It is not open to the public but demonstrates a continuing use of part of the building as an official residence. Originally nine residences were provided for senior officers such as the clerks of the two Houses, and the Speaker's House, which was the largest and finest, alone retains this function.

Although part of it has become offices, and another section has been made into a private flat for the Speaker, the suite of State Rooms on the principal floor is still used for official entertaining and remains much as completed in 1859. The main reception rooms are planned around a glazed cloister and include

ABOVE **The State Rooms are approached from the ground floor by a fine double staircase embellished with brass railings topped with heraldic beasts and gothic candelabra.**

LEFT **Decoration of such rooms as the drawing room was carried out after Pugin's death but following his style. The room has a fine grey marble fireplace, now embellished again with its original brass decorations which were put in store when the fireplace was painted cream earlier this century.**